Lift-the-Flap Book

# EWW! Critter Litter

## See what critters leave behind!

Stan Tekiela

Adventure Publications
Cambridge, Minnesota

Coyote tracks can look a lot like a dog's tracks.

Coyotes eat other animals to survive. You might find a small pile of fur and bones left over from their dinner. Yuck!

# Coyote

If you see a big mound of dirt near a hole in the ground, it could be a coyote den. Coyotes dig a safe, dry home in a hillside for their babies. You might not see signs of a coyote very often. You are more likely to hear them howl at night.

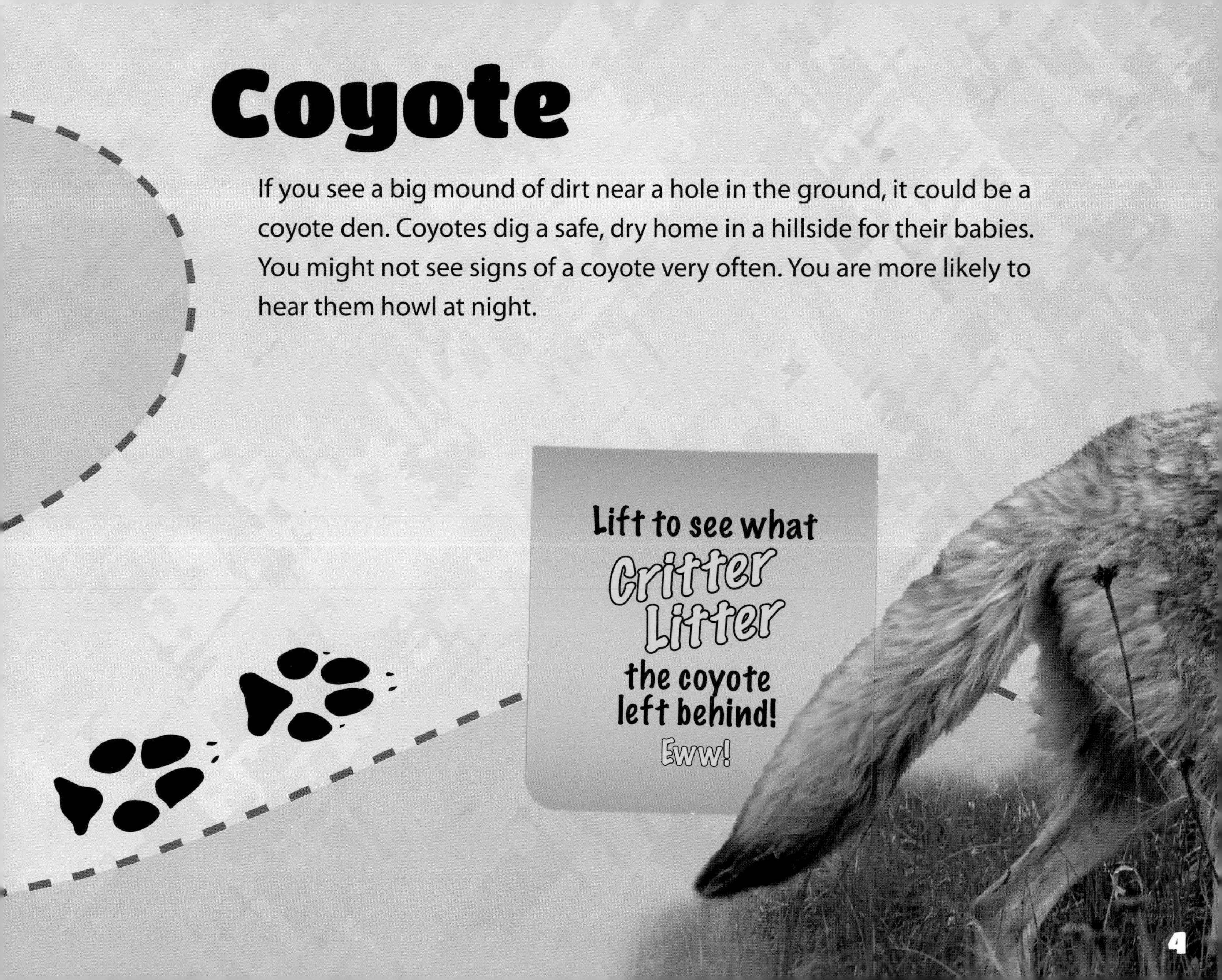

A squirrel collects green leaves for its nest. It weaves them together to make a cozy home. As the leaves dry, they turn brown. To get extra comfy, a squirrel digs into its clump of dry leaves. Look for squirrel nests in the branches of trees, and try to find tracks and other signs they leave behind.

**A squirrel's back feet are bigger than its front feet.**

Squirrel food doesn't come in wrappers. It comes inside nuts. A pile of empty nuts is like a squirrel's garbage can!
Lift to see what
Critter
Litter
the squirrel
left behind!
Eww!

A raccoon's front tracks look a lot like your hands.

If you find half-eaten berries on a log or a rock, they may have been a raccoon's tasty treat.

# Northern Raccoon

Raccoons get food anywhere they can, even from garbage cans! So if your garbage cans are tipped over, a raccoon might have visited your place. To know for sure, look for paw prints.

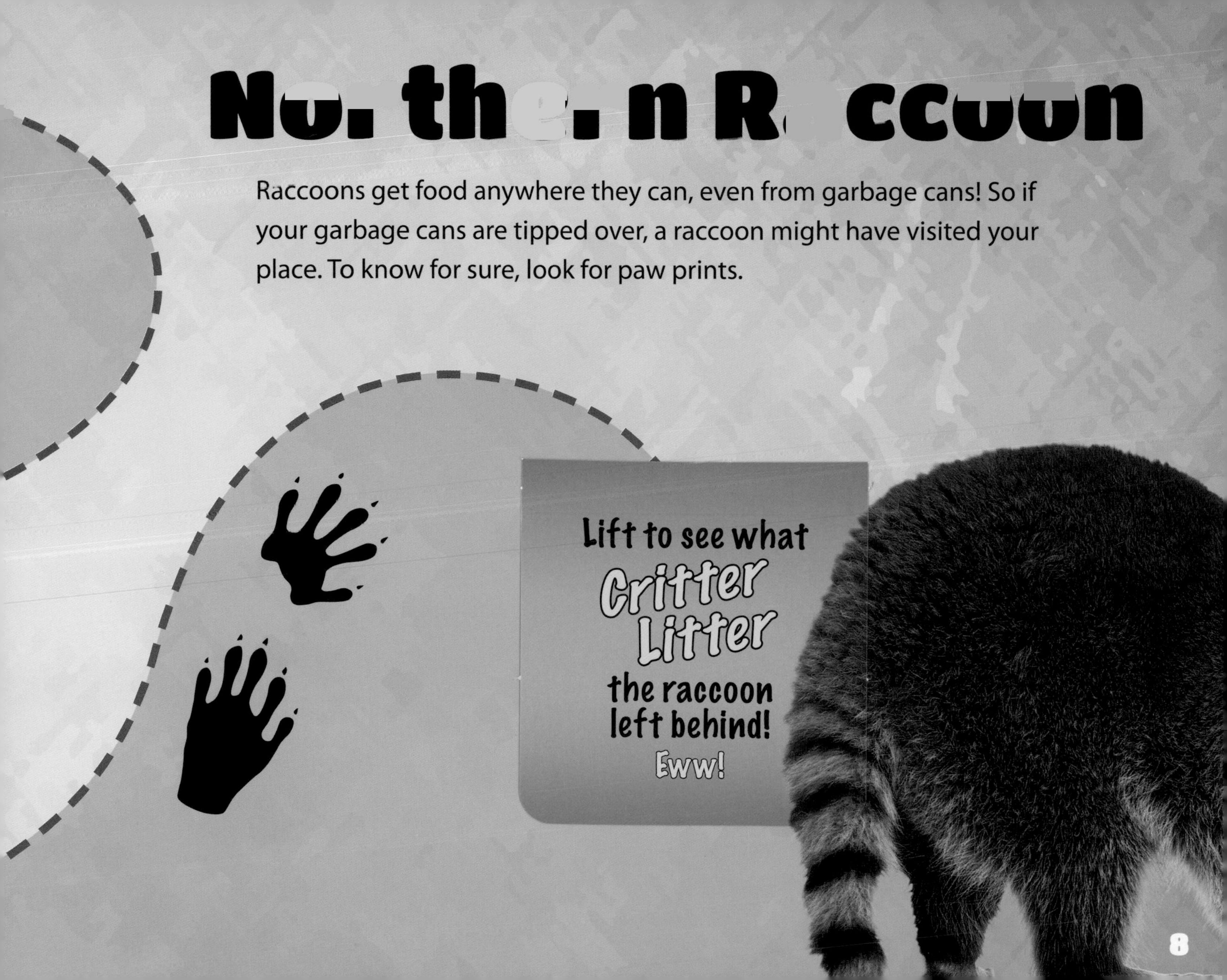

# Virginia Opossum

Opossums are about the size of a house cat. They are unique because the mother carries her babies in a pouch on her belly. If you see an opossum lying in your yard, it might just be scared. Opossums play dead when they are afraid. To find this critter, look for its strange tracks.

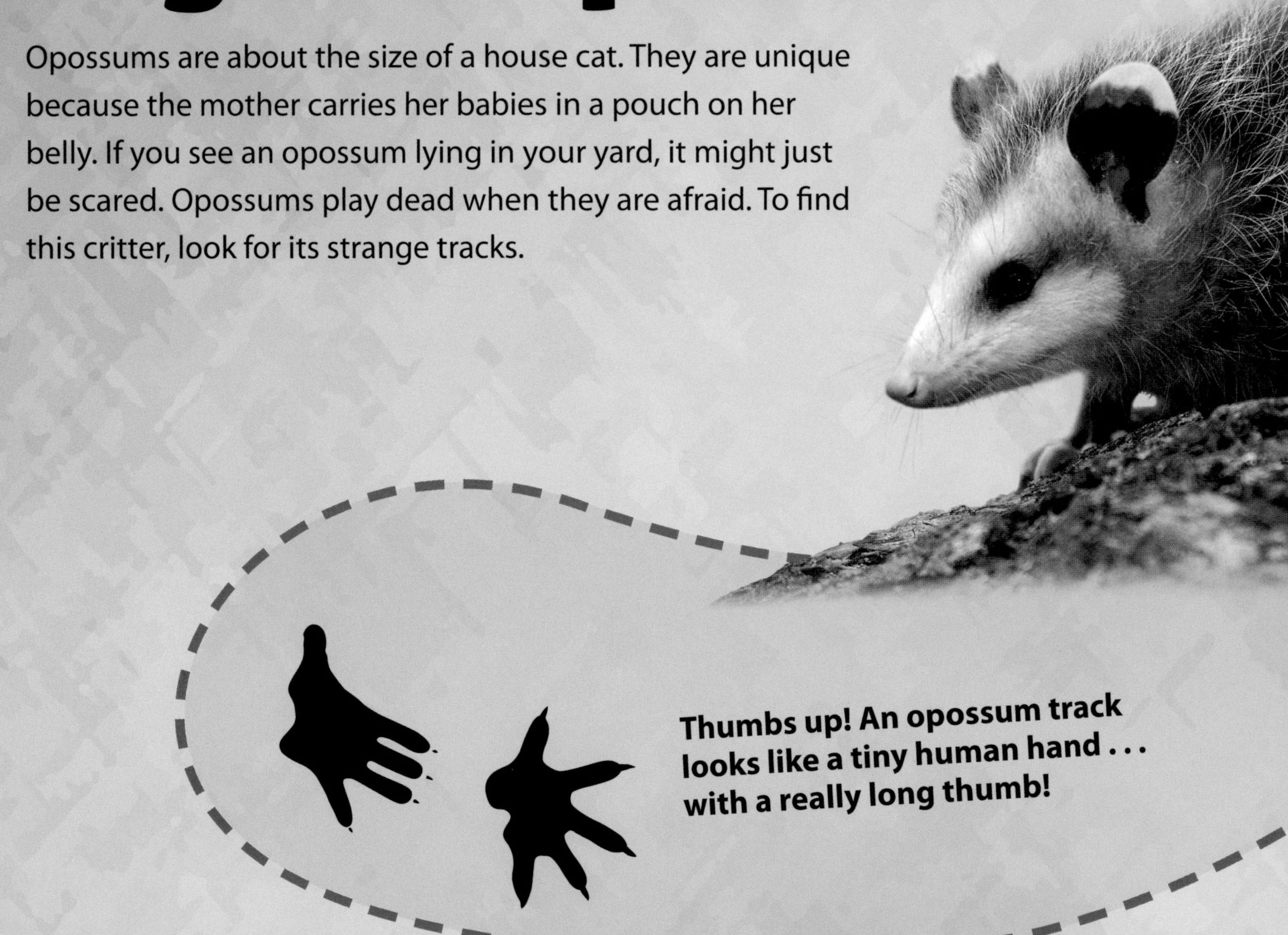

**Thumbs up! An opossum track looks like a tiny human hand . . . with a really long thumb!**

Opossums love sunflower seeds. If your bird feeder is empty, the seeds might have been an opossum's snack!

Lift to see what

Critter Litter

the opossum left behind!

Eww!

Woodchucks walk in grassy places, so their tracks are hard to see. Their back feet have five toes, but their front feet only have four toes. Weird!

If your garden gets chewed up, the plants might have been a woodchuck's dinner salad!

# Woodchuck

If you find a large hole under your garage or barn, a family of woodchucks might be living there! Woodchucks also dig homes into hillsides and under fallen trees. Their homes have a special underground room that woodchucks use as a bathroom.

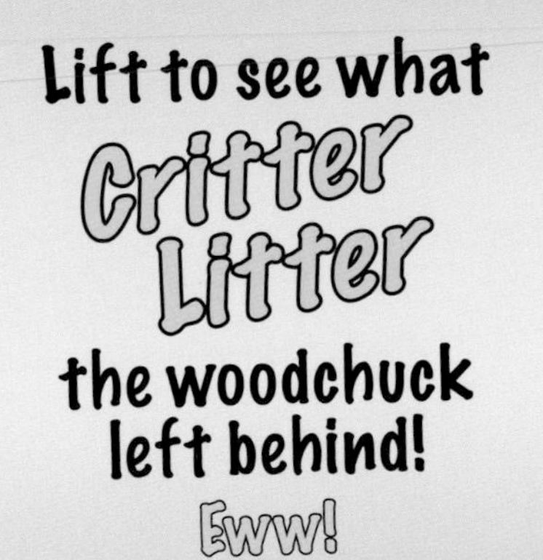

A cougar track is as large as a grown-up's hand.

Cougars don't have refrigerators. They bury their leftovers!

# Cougar

A cougar (also called a mountain lion) has a special way to tell other cougars that it is in the area. It scrapes dirt, twigs and grass into a pile. Then the cougar pees on the pile. Gross! So small piles of stinky dirt are a sign that a cougar is nearby. Cougars are very rare in most parts of the country.

Badgers are famous for being fast diggers. If you see large piles of fresh dirt, a badger den may be close. Badgers eat meat, including small animals such as mice, rats and gophers. Badgers eat outside their dens, so if you find a den, there might be leftovers nearby.

**Who needs a shovel? Each badger toe has a long, sharp claw.**

If you come upon a field with large piles of dirt, a badger might be nearby.

Lift to see what

**Critter Litter**

the badger left behind!

Eww!

Moose tracks look like huge hearts.

Late each winter, bull moose shed their antlers. Look for old antlers on the ground in spring.

# Moose

Moose often leave tracks on dirt roads or along the sides of streams and ponds. Moose are heavy, so their tracks sink into the dirt. If a male moose is in the area, it scrapes bark off small trees to clean and sharpen its antlers. Moose also tear branches from trees as they eat bark.

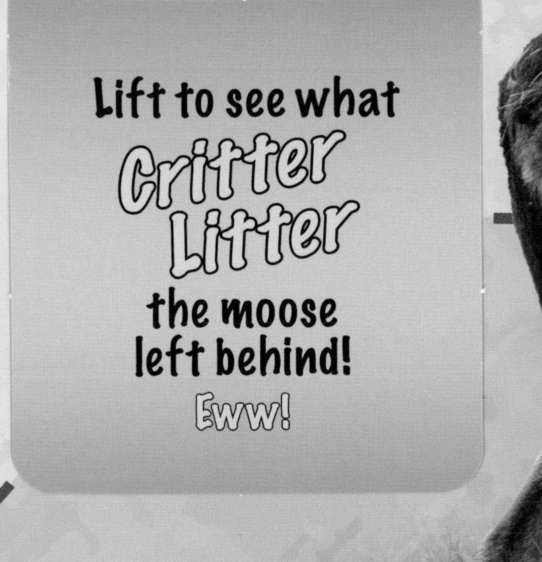

Wolf tracks have four toes on their front and back feet.

Dogs like to chew on bones. So do wolves. If you find a gnawed bone, a wolf might have done it!

# Gray Wolf

Wolves are shy, so seeing one is rare. You might hear one, though. Wolves howl to talk to family members. If you find a giant pile of dirt with a large hole in it, that could be a wolf's den. The holes are very big, but don't climb in! There might be other signs that wolves live there, such as bones and fur. If you find a wolf's den, stay away.

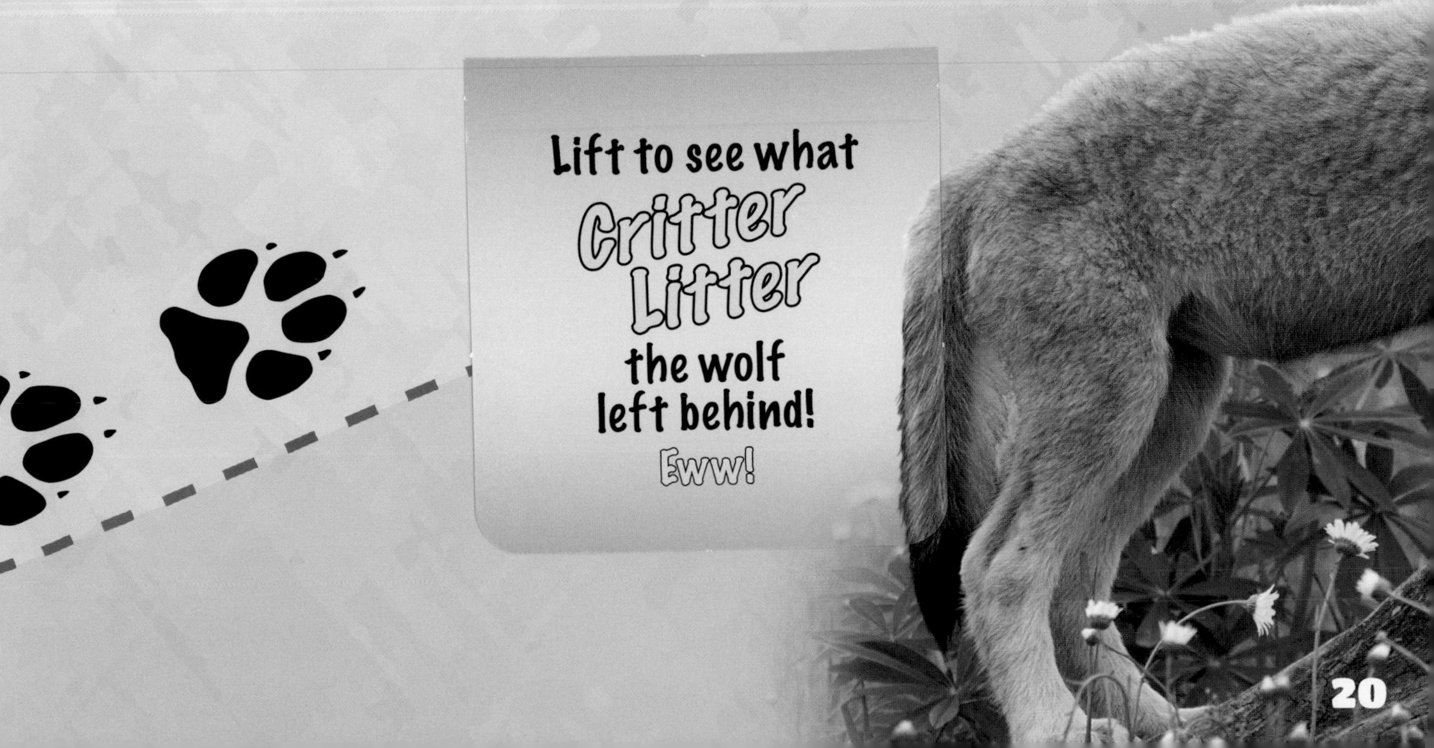

You might not have seen a skunk before, but you have probably smelled one! The strong, stinky smell of their spray is hard to miss. Pew! That's why you should leave a skunk alone if you see one.

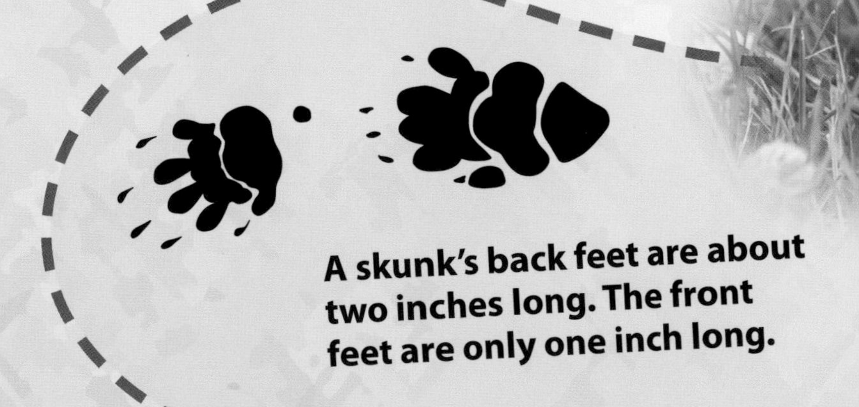

**A skunk's back feet are about two inches long. The front feet are only one inch long.**

If you see a small patch of freshly dug dirt, a skunk might have been looking for worms to eat.

Lift to see what Critter Litter the skunk left behind! Eww!

Bear tracks are huge. Each foot has five toes and claws.

An itchy back? No problem! Bears rub against trees. It leaves fur and special smells behind. This lets other bears know, “I’m here.”

# Black Bear

If you find logs and rocks that are turned over, a bear may have been looking for bugs to eat. Bears also love berries. So if you see a raspberry bush picked clean, it might have been a bear having dessert!

Lift to see what
Critter
Litter
the bear
left behind!
Eww!

# Porcupine

Porcupines climb high in trees to find bark to eat. So trees with missing bark might be a porcupine's dining room! Porcupines also sleep in trees. They only come down when they move to another tree. When they walk, they flatten the grass, so look for their grassy trails.

**Porcupines waddle. Their tracks look like a wide, wiggly line from one tree to another.**